NAVPRESS
Discipleship Inside Out®

NavPress is the publishing ministry of The Navigators, an international Christian organization and leader in personal spiritual development. NavPress is committed to helping people grow spiritually and enjoy lives of meaning and hope through personal and group resources that are biblically rooted, culturally relevant, and highly practical.

For a free catalog go to www.NavPress.com
or call 1.800.366.7788 in the United States or 1.800.839.4769 in Canada.

www.navpress.com
www.studentlifebiblestudy.com

ISBN-13: 978-1-61291-344-5

Cover design by: Katie Beth Owens

Printed in the United States of America

1 2 3 4 5 6 7 8 / 17 16 15 14 13 12

31 verses EVERY TEENAGER SHOULD KNOW

AUDACIOUS

NAVPRESS
Discipleship Inside Out®

TABLE OF CONTENTS

INTRODUCTION

Do you want your life to count?

If we're honest, we have only so much time on this earth. I don't remind us of this to be morbid, but to motivate us. In fact, Scripture reminds us of this reality over and over again. Our lives are a "vapor," a "mist," and "like the grass." We're here one moment and then, just as suddenly, our time is up.

But God's Word never changes. Everything else will fade away, passing like fads and fashions, but God's Word will remain. Forever.

So if we want our lives to count, if we want our time on this planet to matter, we have to set our feet firmly on the unshakable rock of God's Word and lock our eyes on Christ. Don't get distracted. Don't get scared or overwhelmed. God has awesome things in store. He is at work right now, changing your life and changing this world, forever. Nothing will ever be the same again.

Two thousand years ago, a man named Paul had his life transformed when he met Jesus. He went from being one of the Church's fiercest enemies to its boldest hero. The world's first Christians were described as "turning the whole world upside down."

So what has happened since then? When and where did we get so off track?

Why are we settling for such ordinary lives today?

My friends and I hope the devotions in this little book help get you moving in the right direction — toward a life of meaning, purpose, and impact. Spend the next 31 days exploring God's Word to see what Paul meant when he challenged Christ-followers with these words:

"Be on your guard; stand firm in the faith; be courageous; be strong." (1 Corinthians 16:13)

Make the most of your life. Be . . . **AUDACIOUS**.

JEREMY MAXFIELD
Editor

HOW TO USE

Now that you own this incredible little book, you may be wondering, "What do I do with it?"

Glad you asked . . . The great thing about this book is that you can use it just about any way you want.

It's not a system. It's a resource that can be used in ways that are as unique and varied as you are.

A few suggestions . . .

THE "ONE MONTH" PLAN

On this plan, you'll read one devotional each day for a month. This is a great way to immerse yourself in the Bible for a month-long period. (OK, we realize that every month doesn't have 31 days. But 28 or 30 is close enough to 31, right?) The idea is to cover a lot of information in a short amount of time.

THE "SCRIPTURE MEMORY" PLAN

The idea behind this plan is to memorize the verse for each day's devotional; you don't move on to the next devotional until you have memorized the one you're on. If you're like most people, this might take you more than one day per devotional. So, this plan takes a slower approach.

THE "I'M NO WILLIAM SHAKESPEARE" PLAN

Don't like to write or journal? This plan is for you . . . Listen, not everyone expresses themselves the same. If you don't like to express yourself through writing, that's OK. Simply read the devotional for each verse, then read the questions. Think about them. Pray through them. But don't feel like you have to journal if you don't want to.

THE "STRENGTH IN NUMBERS" PLAN

God designed humans for interaction. We are social creatures. How cool would it be if you could go through *31:Audacious* with your friends? Get a group of friends together. Consider agreeing to read five verses each week, then meet to talk about it.

Pretty simple, right? Choose a plan. Or make up your own. But get started already. What are you waiting on?

verse 1

Be on guard! Be alert! You do not know when that time will come.

MARK 13:33

We haven't always had the Internet and cell phones. I know! What did we do? Not only were there no Angry Birds, you couldn't send a text, post a status, tweet, or even call. Messages were sent differently, and high-priority messages needed a special kind of attention, like a warning beacon. The Great Wall of China is probably the most well-known example of this. Let's say you were being attacked. Don't worry: You set up a warning beacon system. You light a fire, which signals the guys at the next station to light their fire, which signals the next guy to light his fire, and so on, until your buddy gets the message and calls in the cavalry to help you out. The catch? The guards had to be waiting and watching at all times.

Two thousand years ago, a guy named John Mark compiled stories from the apostle Peter in what is now the gospel of Mark. His task was to be as true to the events as possible. And in chapter 13, he writes down a warning Jesus shared on the Mount of Olives. Jesus is talking with the disciples about the last days. Toward the end, He reminds the disciples that, while no one knows when the end of times is coming (not even Him), they must remain alert. Take a minute now to read the warning that has been passed down to us in Mark 13:31-37.

The guards on the Great Wall had one job: watching. They didn't get distracted. They didn't sleep on the job. They watched and they waited, never losing focus. Jesus says: Keep awake. Don't fall asleep. Metaphorically speaking, don't get caught napping when I come back. Maybe it sounds extreme to say we all should live our lives as if Jesus is coming back at any moment, but it's true. Are we paying attention?

REFLECT

1. DO YOU THINK IT'S EXTREME TO LIVE OUR LIVES AS IF JESUS IS COMING BACK AT ANY MOMENT?

Yes, sort of

No, because we should always live in a Christ following way no matter what.

2. IF YOU KNEW THAT JESUS WAS RETURNING TOMORROW, HOW WOULD YOU CHANGE YOUR LIFE IN ANTICIPATION?

I would strive to be more holy.

3. WHAT DOES ACTIVELY "WATCHING" FOR JESUS' RETURN LOOK LIKE IN YOUR EVERYDAY LIFE?

holiness, obedience, and courage to follow God.

VERSE TWO

But you are a chosen people, a royal priesthood, a holy nation, God's special possession, that you may declare the praises of him who called you out of darkness into his wonderful light.

1 PETER 2:9

Can you think of something you would spend a lot of money on? An iPad? A car? What about a child? Adoptive parents can spend anywhere from $9,000 to $30,000 in the process of bringing their child home. That's right, $30,000. Why would anyone want to pay that much to adopt a child? Think about this . . . a two-year-old named Grace was living in an orphanage in Moldova (that's near Russia) when she was adopted. Before she was adopted, she was never hugged, she was always sick, and she would hide food in her bed so she would have enough to eat. She was just trying to survive, but when she was chosen for adoption, she was no longer an orphan; her whole life changed.

Open your Bible to 1 Peter 2:9-10. Before you read, let's get a little background information. Peter is writing to Christians who were living within the Roman Empire. The Romans liked to party! Most people celebrated in ways that wouldn't line up with what Christ would have His followers do. Roman Christians wouldn't participate, which made them outcasts. They lost friendships, were made fun of, and were considered weird. Sound familiar? Have you had similar things happen to you? If so, Peter is writing to you!

Now, read 1 Peter 2:9-10. Peter says that Jesus, the Son of God, chose you. Just like Grace's parents chose her, Jesus found you in a sad, sickly state and chose you to love. Not only did He choose you, He allows you to work on His behalf. That is what Peter means when he says you are "a royal priesthood." Grace is allowed to live in her parents' house, eat her parents' food, and do things for her parents. Why? Because she is her parents' daughter, she is a part of them. You are no longer an orphan. You are a part of God's family and you are allowed to act on God's behalf. Now live like it!

REFLECT

1. HOW DOES IT MAKE YOU FEEL TO KNOW THAT GOD HAS CHOSEN YOU?

I feel excited and overwhelmed with joy and gladness.

2. NOW THAT YOU KNOW THAT THE CREATOR OF THE UNIVERSE HAS CHOSEN YOU, WHAT CHANGES DO YOU NEED TO MAKE TO YOUR LIFESTYLE?

I have always known he has chosen me.

Be more aware of God.

3. PETER SAYS LATER IN VERSE 12, "LIVE SUCH GOOD LIVES AMONG THE PAGANS THAT, THOUGH THEY ACCUSE YOU OF DOING WRONG, THEY MAY SEE YOUR GOOD DEEDS AND GLORIFY GOD ON THE DAY HE VISITS US." LIST THREE KIND THINGS YOU CAN DO FOR SOMEONE WHO DOESN'T KNOW GOD SO THEY WILL SEE THAT YOU BELONG TO GOD.

1 Celebrate and Mourn with them,
2 Help them with general stuff,
3 Strive to become their friend!

VERSE 3

I am the LORD, who brought you up out of Egypt to be your God; therefore be holy, because I am holy.

LEVITICUS 11:45

"Like father, like son." It's a phrase with a straightforward message: A son typically copies his father's behavior. But this isn't just a father and son phenomenon. A child, regardless of gender, will adopt the behavior of a parent, whether that's a mom or dad. Children won't mimic every single characteristic of their parents, but they will definitely copy a few things. The simple fact is that both parents pass down certain traits to their children, whether they realize it or not. Children learn certain fears, habits, and beliefs from their parents, and in this way behavior is passed down from generation to generation.

Open your Bible and read Leviticus 11:45. At this point in Scripture, God is giving the Israelites dietary restrictions, telling them what they should and shouldn't eat, so that they can be distinct and separate from the nations that surround them. God tells the Israelites to be holy, because He is holy. *Holy* essentially means to be set apart. Therefore, to be holy as God is holy is to be set apart and free from the sin in this world. And if the Israelites had any doubts as to why they should listen to God, He reminds them that He is the one who rescued them from Egypt. He is God and He is their Savior. This is more than enough reason to follow His lead.

Although believers today don't have to follow these particular dietary restrictions in order to be followers of Christ, we must still be holy, because God is holy. We mimic our parents, so how much more should we mimic our heavenly Father? As we grow in our faith, as we study God's Word and learn more about Him, it is only natural that we begin to take on His character and copy His virtue. Like the Israelites, we ought to be like the God who saved us.

REFLECT

1. WHAT ARE THE AREAS IN YOUR LIFE WHERE GOD'S HOLINESS IS MOST EVIDENT?

The beauty of the universe, and beyond.

2. WHAT ARE THE AREAS IN YOUR LIFE WHERE YOU AREN'T SET APART FROM SIN AS GOD IS SET APART?

When you get frustrated with siblings.
Argue!

3. WHAT STEPS CAN YOU TAKE IN ORDER TO INHERIT MORE OF THE HOLINESS GOD WISHES TO PASS DOWN TO YOU?

1 Pray
2 Obey
3 Believe

VERSE FOUR

Be alert and of sober mind. Your enemy the devil prowls around like a roaring lion looking for someone to devour.

1 Peter 5:8

Have you seen a status like this on Facebook? My profile has been viewed 97 times just today, and I can see I have quite a few observer. Big thanks to the Facebook team for finally giving us something to check our profile views with! Check it out . . . then it gives a link. If you have been on Facebook for a while, you know NOT to click on the link because it's a virus. You know that Facebook can't always be trusted, so you change your passwords from time to time and keep some information private. You know there are people who use the Internet to try to harm you or your computer, so you have learned to be careful.

Read 1 Peter 5:8-9. The Christians whom Peter is writing to live in a culture similar to ours. They face temptations to find happiness in alcohol, sex, or other religions that encourage self-indulgence. In fact, these Christians were being persecuted because they refused to do these things. Peter reminds them that the devil is REAL! And not only is he real but he is waiting for them, looking for ways to ensnare them. They must be careful to avoid being caught in his traps. Peter knows what it's like to fall into the devil's trap. Remember, Peter denied knowing Jesus three times just before Jesus was crucified.

Just as we have to be aware that there are people who want to use the Internet to hurt others, the devil wants to use things that God meant for good to destroy us. We see him in the news when a violent crime has been committed, but do we see him around us? Do you see him in the gossip you are spreading? Do you see him when you lie to your parents about going to a party because your parents "just won't understand"? Remember what Peter says: "Be alert, control yourself! He is out there waiting!"

reflect

1. Examine yourself. What are you doing that is allowing Satan to devour you?

You are thinking bad thoughts, or saying bad words.

2. Spend a few minutes talking with God. Repent and ask for strength to resist the devil's temptation.

Dear Lord, thank you for your strength, and death, defending us from eternal death.

Amen!

3. What are some ways you can be on your guard against the devil?

If you begin to think an evil thought, wipe it away, and start fresh.

verse 5

If you do what is right, will you not be accepted? But if you do not do what is right, sin is crouching at your door; it desires to have you, but you must rule over it.

GENESIS 4:7

Sin and addiction can take many forms. Perhaps most obvious are behaviors involving alcohol and drugs or sex and pornography, but there are other addictions that sometimes slip under the radar. Food, shopping, and media can all become addictions as well. Essentially, addiction is a compulsive need for something. In the beginning, these seemingly harmless things may seem enjoyable, but the moment they become addictions, the moment they have mastery over a person, they become bitter and burdensome.

The word *sin* first appears as a warning in the Bible. Open your Bible now and read about the world's first sibling rivalry in Genesis 4:1-16. Cain and Abel have just brought their offerings to God, but God favors Abel's offering over Cain's. The reason? As the Bible later explains, Abel's offering was presented in faith. When Cain realizes that he hasn't pleased God with his empty religious gesture, he becomes angry. That's when God speaks of sin in Genesis 4:7. God knows the sin that is rising up in Cain's heart, and He warns him not to open the door to it. Sadly, in the next verse we find that Cain flings the door wide open for sin to wreck his life despite God's warning, murdering his brother Abel in a jealous rage.

Some things will simply always be sinful. However, there are some desires in this world that begin innocently but mutate into monstrous addictions. We must, of course, be on our guard against the more obvious sins, but we should also be vigilant against the more subtle types of sin, the ones that begin as simple desires but creep into our hearts, growing into addictions, idols, or wild emotional outbursts. Sin wants to control and destroy us, but we must do what Cain failed to do. We must heed God's warning and guard against the sins preying on us, ready to pounce. Don't be a victim.

REFLECT

1. WHAT ARE THE THINGS THAT YOU DESIRE?

An Ipod
Remodeling my room
e.t.c

2. WHAT ARE SOME DESIRES IN YOUR LIFE THAT OFTEN CONTROL YOU?

electronics !!!!!!!!!!
Music! !!

3. WHAT STEPS CAN YOU TAKE TODAY TO CONTROL YOUR DESIRES AND MASTER THE SIN THAT'S CROUCHING AT THE DOOR?

learn when to "Stop" playing, or listening.

VERSE SIX

Then he said to them, "Watch out! Be on your guard against all kinds of greed; life does not consist in an abundance of possessions."

LUKE 12:15

One of the most repugnant and truly awful characters ever to grace a movie screen has got to be Veruca Salt. Just her name rubs you the wrong way, right? Veruca Salt is one of the children who wins a golden ticket into Willy Wonka's Chocolate Factory, and never has there been a more spoiled and rotten child. Veruca's father is filthy rich, and she gets whatever she wants. But when she's denied by Wonka inside the factory, she breaks into a song about how she wants the world, give it to her, she wants it now. She's truly horrible.

Interestingly enough, Jesus had something to say about the Veruca Salts of this world. Luke describes a scene in which a man asks Jesus to settle a family inheritance dispute. Jesus answers with a parable about a rich farmer who worried about storing up more and more goods for his own consumption. When he died, what had he really accomplished by hording his wealth? When God called upon him for his soul, possessions were meaningless. Jesus warns against wanting everything you see because your life can only mean so much when it's wrapped up in things. Read the story now in Luke 12:13-21.

Although Veruca Salt is a fictional character, we know that it really is easy to become obsessed with getting more of whatever we want. Things like phones and clothes and cars aren't bad in their own right, but when we base our worth (and the worth of others) on that materialistic scale, we will be found empty upon leaving this world. At the end of the parable, Jesus reminds His listeners that those who are "rich toward God" are the ones who truly have it all. Veruca Salt's demise came when a scale tipped, deeming her rotten with greed, and dropped her down a trash chute. Maybe we should take inventory of our own attitudes, so we too don't end up as bad eggs.

REFLECT

1. WHY IS IT SO HARD FOR US TO GUARD OURSELVES AGAINST THE MATERIALISTIC WAYS OF THE WORLD?

Because every where we go the ways of the world are there.

2. WHAT DO YOU THINK IT MEANS TO BE "RICH TOWARD GOD"?

You act like God is not important, and your riches will save you, and get you anything

3. WHAT PRACTICAL STEPS CAN YOU TAKE TO DEFEND YOURSELF AGAINST WANTING IT ALL?

hang w/ the right crowd
be diligent in how you spend your money

VERSE 7

Do not repay anyone evil for evil. Be careful to do what is right in the eyes of everyone.

ROMANS 12:17

Imagine this: A boy gets home from school to find that his dog has torn up couch pillows, ripped up newspapers, and just made a really huge mess. The boy, in his anger, runs through the house knocking over picture frames and kicking over chairs. The boy's mom returns home from work to find the mess and asks her son what happened. He responds by saying that he found the dog's mess when he got home and decided to get back at the dog by making it bigger. Sounds ridiculous, right?

Look at Romans 12:10-20. It's clear from Paul's letter to the church in Rome that he was looking forward to visiting them. However, there was growing tension in Rome, and a lot of aggression was mounting against the church. When Paul finally arrived in Rome, it was as a prisoner. Paul didn't try to get even with his captors. Instead, we see in Scripture that Paul spent every opportunity sharing the love of Christ with them. Paul trusted in God as both judge and provider of salvation. Although his situation was unjust, Paul continued to trust that God was in control and would one day make things right, all the while hoping for the salvation of everyone he encountered, including his captors. He may have been imprisoned, but Paul continued believing in the importance of living in peace with those around him.

Repaying evil for evil makes even less sense than our story about the boy and his dog. As absurd as the story was, it makes a clear point: When we attempt to repay evil for evil, all we are doing is making a bigger mess. Whereas if we trust in God as the judge, as Paul did throughout his lifetime, we will find ourselves doing what is right, even in the most difficult of circumstances.

REFLECT

1. WHAT ARE SOME WAYS IN WHICH REVENGE, OR REPAYING EVIL FOR EVIL, REVEALS A LACK OF FAITH IN GOD?

God has no evil, and we are to be like God.

2. THINK OF A SPECIFIC SITUATION IN WHICH YOU'RE TEMPTED TO DO WRONG OR GET BACK AT SOMEONE. HOW CAN YOU REVEAL YOUR FAITH BY DOING WHAT IS RIGHT IN THAT SITUATION?

When someone cheats off you, instead of announcing it to the whole world, you keep quiet and speak to them in private.

3. WRITE DOWN THE NAMES OF PEOPLE WHO HAVE WRONGED YOU, AND THEN PRAY THAT GOD WOULD GIVE YOU THE FAITH TO FORGIVE THEM, JUST AS HE HAS FORGIVEN YOU.

Tabitha Mahaffey

I pray you will help me to forgive her just as you forgave me.

VERSE EIGHT

This is a trustworthy saying. And I want you to stress these things, so that those who have trusted in God may be careful to devote themselves to doing what is good. These things are excellent and profitable for everyone.

Titus 3:8

In the 1950s and 1960s, the U.S. Marshals had some interesting assignments. Desegregation was happening, and President Kennedy called in these guys to carry out the Supreme Court's order of allowing blacks into what were formerly known as white schools. The job of the U.S. Marshal was to escort black children through the racially charged hate mobs that sought to discourage (using the word lightly) them from getting in the building. People threw trash, rocks, and lit cigarettes at them, but they had one goal: guard against what is bad and make way for what is right.

Flip over to Titus 3:8 and read. Paul is writing to Titus as a kind of reminder. His letter is short in words, but not on instruction. Being on your guard is twofold. Yes, you have to constantly work to keep the bad stuff out. Denying yourself, not watching that movie, not listening to those songs, praying against gossip and lying and stealing. It's definitely about keeping the bad out. But, just like the U.S. Marshal, you also have to get the good stuff in. As believers, we're about devoting ourselves to good works, not just walking around with a big chip on our shoulders all the time because we're always saying no.

Paul reminds Titus to do the things that profit everyone, to create a community of people who do good works for people who need them. It's not just about saying no; you also have to say yes. For believers, being known as the people who are always denying themselves is one thing, but being known as the people who say yes to helping, to assisting, to befriending, to caring — that is something everyone can get on board with. A good guard knows how to keep out the bad, bringing in what's good instead.

reflect

1. Why is it easy to focus on the negatives, all the things you can't do or have, as a believer?

We must not loath them, and focus on hate!

2. What are some of the bad things that you should be on guard about?

homosexuals

3. What are some tangible ways you and your community can get the good stuff in?

Gods WORD

verse 9

Be careful not to practice your righteousness in front of others to be seen by them. If you do, you will have no reward from your Father in heaven.

MATTHEW 6:1

The evangelist Dwight L. Moody once said, "Character is what you are in the dark." Put a different way, your character is defined as what you do when no one is looking. You may be kind and obedient toward your mother when others are watching, but behind the walls of your home, maybe you're defiant and rude. That would mean your image (what others see) is good, but your character (what only you see, and in this case, your mother sees) is lacking.

Jesus had something to say about character in Matthew 6:1, so grab your Bible and read that passage. Matthew 6 is smack in the middle of the Sermon on the Mount, one of Jesus' most famous teaching moments. A crowd is gathered around Him, and He takes time to remind them that when you do good deeds just so everyone else around you will see them and think you're great, that's it. That moment is as much of a reward as you'll get. Because you made sure everyone was looking, you missed out on the greater blessing. Your image is good, but your character is lacking.

God cares about the person you are when only He is looking. He cares about what's in your heart. He wants you to check your motives. Are you obedient toward your mother because He asked you to be, because you love Him? Or is it because that person you think is cute is watching? The thing about honing your image is that it's a lie. You can't take it with you to heaven, and God will only want to hear about your character. Of course, sometimes you can't avoid being seen when you do the right or just thing, but your heart should be turned toward pleasing God, not showing off for people.

REFLECT

1. WHAT IS THE DIFFERENCE BETWEEN IMAGE AND CHARACTER?

2. WHY IS IT HARD TO DO THE RIGHT THING EVEN WHEN NO ONE ELSE IS WATCHING?

3. ARE YOU MORE CONCERNED WITH YOUR IMAGE OR YOUR CHARACTER? HOW CAN YOU SPECIFICALLY ASK GOD TO HELP YOU BE MORE CONCERNED WITH RIGHTEOUS DEEDS DONE IN QUIET?

VERSE TEN

Watch your life and doctrine closely. Persevere in them, because if you do, you will save both yourself and your hearers.

1 TIMOTHY 4:16

Is there someone you "like"? Have you driven yourself crazy trying to get that person to notice you? Let me guess . . . you've dressed in your favorite outfit, put on some cologne or perfume, "liked" all of their Facebook statuses, followed them on Twitter, and texted them several times a day. If that's not working, maybe you should touch their arm. Psychologists have performed experiments with touch in which they had boys ask girls out on dates. Boys who for two seconds lightly touched the arm of the girl they were asking out got more dates than the ones who didn't. A little thing like touch can make a huge difference.

Read 1 Timothy 4:9-16. Timothy is a young guy who is put in charge of a church with a lot of problems. Some people in the church didn't want to listen to him because he was young. Now Timothy could have tried impressing these people by saying all the right things, praying the right way, and wearing the right stuff. But, just like a touch on the arm can be more effective in getting you a date, Paul tells Timothy that little things can be more effective in pointing people to Christ.

You're kind of like Timothy. You may not be in charge of a church, but people are looking at you for guidance whether you know it or not. Especially if people know that you're a Christian. People are watching you and looking to see Jesus in you. Now you could say a lot of religious words or always wear Christian shirts or pray loudly in the lunchroom, but Paul is telling you to focus on the little things. Just like touching an arm could get you a date, a little thing like saying hello to that kid who sits by himself at lunch can begin to show Jesus to him. What you do matters, and it is often the little things you do that matter the most.

REFLECT

1. WHAT ARE SOME THINGS YOU DO THAT DO NOT REFLECT JESUS?

Get frusterated
Lie
Steal-minor things

2. LIST THREE PEOPLE YOU KNOW WHO NEED TO KNOW ABOUT JESUS.

3. FOR EACH OF THESE PEOPLE, WRITE DOWN ONE WAY YOU CAN SHOW THEM JESUS TODAY.

Kindness
Love
Joy
Mercy

VERSE 11

Whatever happens, conduct yourselves in a manner worthy of the gospel of Christ. Then, whether I come and see you or only hear about you in my absence, I will know that you stand firm in one Spirit, striving together as one for the faith of the gospel.

PHILIPPIANS 1:27

If you want to play an instrument for a professional symphony, you've got to have a little something special. It's not just that you need to be able to play your instrument well, and it's not even that you take conduction well. In order to be part of a symphony, an instrumentalist must be able to play well with others. They have to learn to blend with their section. Anyone can be a solo artist, but it's the mark of true professionals who love the music they play more than individual accolades to play as one.

Open up to Philippians 1:27 and read that verse. Paul writes to the Philippians that he wants to come see them, but he's not sure if he'll be able to. He reminds them that, either way, he wants them to act like they've got the Good News of Jesus (which they do), so that whether he comes to visit or not, he'll know that they play together as one in the Symphony of Christ. Paul wants these believers to be one in spirit, just as each section sounds like only one instrument when played properly. When there is discord, the whole piece is thrown off. The audience can only focus on what's wrong, rather than all the other right that is happening. The same is true with the church Paul is writing to.

Community within the body is not only good and helpful and uplifting, it's mandated. No one is saying be a hermit, or don't talk to anyone who isn't a believer, but the camaraderie and fellowship that you're blessed with is second to none. When you are in deep relationships with other Christians, you have someone to hold you accountable, who will keep you on beat with the symphony. Surround yourself with those people who are playing the music harmoniously, and nonbelievers will wonder what your bond is all about.

REFLECT

1. WHAT DOES IT MEAN TO LIVE YOUR LIFE IN A MANNER WORTHY OF THE GOSPEL?

Living in God's image

2. WHY DO WE SOMETIMES WANT TO DISTANCE OURSELVES FROM OTHER BELIEVERS?

We think they might be very judgemental

3. WHO ARE SOME PEOPLE YOU CAN BE INTENTIONAL ABOUT BUILDING FRIENDSHIPS WITH AS A MEMBER OF THE BODY OF CHRIST?

Serena
My family

VERSE TWELVE

So, if you think you are standing firm, be careful that you don't fall!
1 Corinthians 10:12

The New York Giants beat the New England Patriots for the second time at Super Bowl XLVI in 2012. Eli Manning, the Giants quarterback, won the Super Bowl MVP for the second time (one of only five quarterbacks to do this in NFL history). He also set a Super Bowl record for throwing nine consecutive completions at the start of the game. Eli Manning is a great quarterback. You might say it is in his blood. His father, Archie Manning, was a great NFL quarterback and his brother, Peyton Manning, is a great NFL quarterback. Eli is part of a dynasty of great quarterbacks, but that is not what makes him great. He constantly practices during both the regular season and the off-season to perfect his timing with his receivers. Practice is what keeps him playing in the NFL and playing well.

Read 1 Corinthians 10:1-13. Jesus' sacrifice on the cross allows us to have a loving, personal relationship with God. In Corinth, some Christians were sinning all they wanted because they thought, *Hey, God loves me. He forgives me. We're cool!* They felt entitled to God's grace. Paul says, "Remember who this God is that you are in a relationship with. He is a loving, generous, and forgiving God, but He's not stupid." God knows we need to listen and obey as we walk with Him because He is the only one who can completely cure us of sin.

Eli Manning would be crazy to think that being his father's son alone would make him a great quarterback. Paul is telling us that it is daily listening and following Christ that form our relationship with Him. God is not our "get out of hell free" pass. God is our Creator and Savior whom we desperately need. Stay close to Him and He will change you into something wonderful.

reflect

1. Some couples have a DTR (*Define The Relationship*) talk to know where they are in the relationship. Define your relationship with Christ right now.

an on - off relationship that needs to be strengthened

2. Have you been neglecting your relationship with Christ? Spend some time being honest with Him about why you've been neglecting Him.

Yes, I always forget to pray + spend time w/ God

3. What are some things in your life that you need to practice so your relationship with Christ becomes stronger?

prayer
love
bible reading

verse 13

Therefore, since we have been justified through faith, we have peace with God through our Lord Jesus Christ, through whom we have gained access by faith into this grace in which we now stand. And we boast in the hope of the glory of God.

ROMANS 5:1-2

In Suzanne Collins' best-selling book series The Hunger Games, a girl named Katniss is forced to enter a gladiator-like competition called the Hunger Games. The story takes place in the future, at a time when children are forced to fight one another for public amusement. One of the main pieces of instruction Katniss receives while preparing for the Hunger Games is to do whatever her trainers tell her to do. Sometimes their instructions seem ridiculous, even impossible, but Katniss obeys and in the end discovers that it's because of her trainers and their work in her life that she is able to survive the dangerous and grueling competition.

Paul was constantly battling against the idea of works-based salvation, which claims that someone must be good, do the right things, follow the Law, and in doing so earn their salvation. Romans 5:1-2 is one of many passages in which Paul lays it out clear and simple: Salvation isn't something we do on our own. When Paul says that we have been justified through faith, he is saying that we have trusted in Jesus to do on our behalf what we could never accomplish on our own, namely to make us right before God.

Because of Katniss's faith in her trainers, she is able to survive the dangerous Hunger Games. Similarly, it is only our faith in Christ that reconciles us to God. To rely on anything else besides God's grace and our faith in Him would be to sabotage our relationship with the living God. He has made a way for us to enjoy peace with Him through Jesus, and now we are left with the option of trusting in Him. Unlike the Hunger Games, the decision to trust Jesus is about more than just survival — no matter how you slice it, our time on this planet is brief. A decision to trust Christ is about the reality of our eternal relationship with the Creator.

REFLECT

1. ASK YOURSELF WHOM OR WHAT YOU RELY ON TO FEEL LIKE YOUR LIFE IS "RIGHT." ARE YOU MORE INTERESTED IN JUSTIFYING YOUR LIFE BY YOUR FRIENDS' STANDARDS OR IN BEING MADE RIGHT (JUSTIFIED) BY GOD'S GRACE?

2. THINK ABOUT THE TIME YOU FIRST PUT YOUR FAITH IN CHRIST, BEGINNING A RIGHT RELATIONSHIP WITH GOD. IF YOU HAVE NEVER DONE THIS, WILL YOU DO IT NOW? IF YOU HAVE, ARE YOU LIVING LIKE IT?

3. WHAT ARE SOME WAYS YOU CAN REMIND YOURSELF DAILY OF THE PEACE IN THIS LIFE AND IN HEAVEN MADE POSSIBLE ONLY THROUGH JESUS?

VERSE FOURTEEN

Examine yourselves to see whether you are in the faith; test yourselves. Do you not realize that Christ Jesus is in you — unless, of course, you fail the test?

2 CORINTHIANS 13:5

Larry Osborne, pastor of North Coast Church in Vista, California, often says, "Bibles are far too often used as binoculars instead of mirrors." For example, maybe you've heard or said something like: "Doesn't she know she shouldn't dress that way in church?" or "Why is he coming to church? He's the kind who gives Christians a bad name." Are you guilty of using the Bible to condemn others?

Read 2 Corinthians 13:5. Some of the Corinthian Christians were "do-gooders." It was easy for them to say no to some of the "big" sins, and they didn't understand why others would sin. Some of the Corinthian Christians were "strugglers." It was a challenge for them not to sin, and they thought the "do-gooders" were too stuck up. So there was a lot of finger pointing going around (some fingers were even pointed at Paul). So Paul wrote them this note to remind them that the gospel of Jesus Christ should humble us. And there is no room to point fingers.

Paul's message is the same for us today. Some of us find it fairly easy to be good. Some of us have a more difficult time toeing the line between following Christ and following the world. Regardless of whether we identify ourselves with the "do-gooders" or the "strugglers," we often use the Bible as binoculars to point out the flaws of those around us. We forget that the Bible is a mirror, which shows us the truth about ourselves (and it isn't always pretty). You are a work in progress! So is everyone else! Make sure you are examining yourself. Love and pray for those who struggle more than you. God is faithful to see what He's started through to completion . . . including you and everyone else who follows Him.

REFLECT

1. WHEN YOU EXAMINE YOUR LIFE, DO YOU TRUST CHRIST MORE OR DO YOU TRUST YOURSELF MORE?

2. WHO ARE SOME PEOPLE YOU HAVE SEEN THROUGH YOUR BIBLICAL BINOCULARS AND JUDGED THEIR SINS WITHOUT JUDGING YOUR OWN? SPEND SOME TIME BEING HONEST WITH GOD AND TELL HIM WHEN YOU HAVE DONE THIS. YOU MAY WANT TO WRITE THIS DOWN.

3. WHAT ARE SOME WAYS YOU CAN SHOW CHRIST TO THE "STRUGGLERS" YOU SEE?

VERSE 15

Immediately the boy's father exclaimed, "I do believe; help me overcome my unbelief!"

MARK 9:24

There's a famous song by Cheap Trick called "I Want You to Want Me," about a young man's plea for a lady to love him. Romantic, no? Isn't this always the case? We want our significant other to WANT to listen to our favorite band, not for us to force it on them. We want our siblings to WANT to unload the dishwasher, not for us to make them do it.

Find Mark 9 in your Bible. We're going to concentrate on verse 24, but read that whole section. Jesus had just come down from the mountain where He had been transfigured, meaning a few of His disciples got a sneak preview of His eternal glory, right into this scene with the father and his little boy, possessed by a demon. Kind of a harsh crash back to reality. The father asks Jesus for help, and Jesus replies, "Everything is possible for one who believes." The man cries out, "I do believe; help me overcome my unbelief!" There is probably a lot we could learn from this man — simply, asking Jesus to help you in all aspects of your faith.

Sometimes, it's difficult to want Jesus enough. Because a lot of our material and physical needs are taken care of, we don't know how to depend on Him daily. We talk about Him, but we don't want Him. We read our Bibles, but we don't need Him. Even if you just want to want Jesus, even if you just want to stop sinning in that one way, even if you just want to want to care about some other aspect of being a follower of Jesus, that's enough to start with. Pray fervently every day that God will help your "want to want" move to a true desire. He's the only one who can truly change your heart.

REFLECT

1. WHAT ARE SOME ASPECTS OF YOUR FAITH THAT YOU "WANT TO WANT" TO CHANGE?

2. WRITE OUT A PRAYER ASKING JESUS TO HELP YOU WANT TO CHANGE THESE THINGS. WHAT ARE YOU ASKING HIM SPECIFICALLY?

3. DO YOU TRULY BELIEVE THE STATEMENT THAT JESUS MAKES IN CHAPTER 9: "EVERYTHING IS POSSIBLE FOR ONE WHO BELIEVES"? WHY OR WHY NOT?

VERSE SIXTEEN

He was a good man, full of the Holy Spirit and faith, and a great number of people were brought to the Lord.

Acts 11:24

The Salvation Army is a worldwide Christian foundation that provides assistance to those battling addictions, suffering as a result of natural disasters, and living in poverty. The British preacher William Booth founded the Salvation Army in 1865. William had a falling-out with church leaders in England because, rather than preaching in a traditional fashion from the pulpit of a church building, he chose to take the gospel to thieves and prostitutes in the streets. William was often attacked in the press, and one day his son, Bramwell, showed him an article that criticized his ministry. William responded, "Fifty years hence it will matter very little indeed how these people treated us; it will matter a great deal how we dealt with the work of God."

Open your Bible and read Acts 11:24. At this point in the Church's history, the gospel of Jesus was beginning to be preached to the Gentiles. This made some people furious, but when the church in Jerusalem heard about Gentiles coming to Christ, they sent Barnabas to look into the matter. After Barnabas arrived in Antioch, he encouraged the new Gentile believers to hold on to their faith in Jesus, which would make sense because his name meant "son of encouragement." Barnabas was known as a man of faith, but he didn't keep his faith to himself. His faith was contagious, and by the end of his stay in Antioch, more people had come to faith in Christ than when he had arrived.

William Booth didn't please all of the religious leaders of his time and Barnabas certainly had his run-ins with people who didn't agree with him, but both men were more concerned about the work of God than the opinions of others. Both Barnabas and William Booth built reputations as men of faith, and they are known to this day as men who were filled with the Holy Spirit.

reflect

1. When people think about you, what likely comes to their mind?

2. How has your reputation changed since you put your faith in Christ?

3. In what ways are you intentionally giving over your reputation to the Lord?

verse 17

For we live by faith, not by sight.

2 CORINTHIANS 5:7

Do you have a dream car? Why do you love that car so much? Is it the way it looks, how fast you can drive it, how cool you would look in it? But . . . do you know how it works? If you popped the hood, could you name every part of the engine and describe what each one does? For most of us the answer is probably no. Does it bother you that you don't know exactly how your dream car works? Of course not! All you care about is getting in the driver's seat and taking off. Every time you get into a car, you have to trust that the car will work and that it is safe. You put your faith in the people who made your car even though you've never seen them.

One of the hardest things about following Jesus is that we have never physically seen Him. There are millions of images of Him (Google "pictures of Jesus Christ" and it will give you 179 million results) but no actual photographs. Read 2 Corinthians 5:7. Paul is well aware of our inability to see Jesus, but he tells us that this temporary blindness should not discourage us from knowing and trusting Christ.

Why should it be discouraging? We ride in cars without seeing or knowing how they work. We eat food at restaurants without seeing the chef. We are blind to a lot of things, yet we put our trust in them. Why then are we so hesitant to trust in Christ? Your car will fail you and you will have a bad meal from time to time, but Christ will never fail you. Though you have never seen Christ with your eyes, you have seen His work in you. You have felt Him and desire to know Him. Keep going. He is more trustworthy than anything you can see.

REFLECT

1. IS GOD GUIDING YOU DOWN A PATH YOU ARE SCARED TO TAKE? IT MAY BE SOMETHING BIG OR SOMETHING LITTLE. WHAT SCARES YOU ABOUT GOING IN THAT DIRECTION?

2. SPEND A FEW MINUTES WRITING DOWN SOME WAYS THAT GOD HAS PROVEN HIMSELF TO BE TRUSTWORTHY AS YOU HAVE WALKED WITH HIM.

3. WHAT IS STOPPING YOU FROM TRUSTING CHRIST COMPLETELY? WRITE DOWN YOUR DOUBTS AND PRAY THAT GOD WILL GIVE YOU STRENGTH TO FOLLOW HIM EVEN WHEN YOU ARE AFRAID.

VERSE EIGHTEEN

Very truly I tell you, whoever believes in me will do the work I have been doing, and they will do even greater things than these, because I am going to the Father.

JOHN 14:12

Throughout history, many people have trained as apprentices. Apprentices learn a craft with a master, someone who really knows what they're doing, a person who has been at it for years. People like Vincent van Gogh, Benjamin Franklin, and even Henry Ford were once peons, trying to learn as much as they could from someone better. Obviously, this group of folks surpassed their teachers. They did more than the people who taught them.

Read John 14:12. Now read it again. Are you in shock? Jesus is saying something pretty revolutionary here. In John 14, Jesus has just finished washing His disciples feet, and the time has almost come for Him to be arrested and crucified. Tensions are high, and Jesus is speaking some of His final words to His small group of followers. He says, "Very truly I tell you, whoever believes in me will do the work I have been doing, and they will do even greater things than these, because I am going to the Father." Did you catch it? Jesus said that those who have faith in Him will do greater things than what He has done, because He was about to leave.

Whoa.

God wants to do amazing things through you — things that glorify Him and lift up His name. He wants you to be a part. He's only asking that you have faith, and sometimes that's the hardest part. We want to be in control of our own lives because we think we know best. Jesus is saying here that if you will only have faith, if you will only let Him steer the course of your life, He's prepared to do incredible works in you. If Jesus healed the sick and the blind and the lame, what does He have in store for you? Trust His Spirit to work in great ways through you today.

REFLECT

1. WHAT DO YOU THINK JESUS MEANT WHEN HE SAID THAT THOSE WHO HAVE FAITH WOULD DO GREATER THINGS THAN HE DID?

2. WHAT DO YOU BELIEVE GOD WANTS TO DO THROUGH YOU?

3. WHAT IS AN OBSTACLE THAT YOU THINK MIGHT HINDER HIM FROM DOING THAT THING?

VERSE 19

But now, this is what the LORD says — he who created you, Jacob, he who formed you, Israel: "Do not fear, for I have redeemed you; I have summoned you by name; you are mine."

ISAIAH 43:1

As of 2011, more than 27 million people in the world are considered slaves. Maybe you think that slavery (especially in America) is something that died out at the end of the Civil War, but you would be wrong. While not as obvious as it used to be, people all over the globe are forced to work for others for free, making them slaves. Young children are bought and sold, girls are forced into the sex trade for money, and those who can't pay their debts are obligated to work to pay them off — sometimes forever. They have little hope of their circumstances ever changing because they need someone to save them. They can't do it themselves.

Open up to Isaiah 43:1 and read that verse. Read it again. What does it say to you? You've probably never been a slave in real life, but we've all been slaves spiritually. The life of the Spirit is hard, mostly because we're slaves to our flesh. We want to feel good by doing the things that we want to do, and it turns out we are the worst masters to serve. But Isaiah 43:1 gives us great hope. We have been redeemed from ourselves, from a life void of God. He has made us, and we are His.

We have been saved. We are no longer slaves, and we belong to someone. There is nothing more hopeful than the statement in Isaiah 43:1, and even though it's in the Old Testament, it points to the future, to Christ dying for our sins and redeeming us from death. That is powerful, supernatural stuff, and the Holy Spirit inhabits our lives to live that truth out. If you ever feel like you don't belong or you're not worthy, keep Isaiah 43:1 in your pocket to remind you that you have been made by someone and you have been saved.

REFLECT

1. WHAT DOES IT MEAN TO BE A SLAVE TO SIN?

2. WHAT ARE SOME SINS THAT YOU IN PARTICULAR FEEL LIKE YOU STRUGGLE WITH?

3. WHAT DOES IT MEAN TO BE REDEEMED? DO YOU FEEL LIKE YOU NEED TO BE SAVED?

VERSE TWENTY

Therefore, since we have such a hope, we are very bold.
2 Corinthians 3:12

Have you ever noticed salesmen on TV? These guys use a method of selling called "the pitch." They are loud, they are bold, and sometimes they are convincing. Does God want us to be salesmen for Christ? If you were "selling" Christ, your pitch might sound something like this: "Are you feeling hot? Worried about hell? You can be safe from hell and go to heaven with Jesus Christ! All you have to do is say a prayer and come to church, and YOU too can have heaven. If you act today, then I will give you three FREE passes to the next Christian concert of your choice." This in-your-face approach to sharing Christ is bold, but are we to be salesmen of Christ?

The boldness that Paul tells us we should have is not an outward, fake boldness. Read 2 Corinthians 3:17-18. Paul is talking about how the light of God shone so brightly on Moses' face when he came down the mountain after receiving the Ten Commandments that he had to cover his face. Now that is amazing! But Paul says what we have, as Christians, is even more impressive. Moses encountered the Spirit of God on the mountain, but we have that same Spirit IN us because of Jesus! That means God's light shines through us from the inside out. Christ shines through you in everything you do — not just on your face.

You don't have to develop a high-energy, in-your-face kind of pitch. The light that Christ has put in you will shine when you act in accordance to God's plan for you. When you show kindness to a stranger, when you forgive your enemies, when you don't spread gossip or dissension — all of these actions make your light shine! This boldness comes from the hope that is in you.

reflect

1. How can you be bold in showing the hope of Christ that is in you?

2. Who do you need to show Christ's hope to today?

3. What is a way you can share Christ with this person?

verse 21

So keep up your courage, men, for I have faith in God that it will happen just as he told me.

ACTS 27:25

People often give meteorologists a hard time because they occasionally get things wrong. Consider, for instance, when the weatherman stands on camera delivering the weekly weather report and forecasts a snow day. People go to bed that evening and dream about making snowmen, sledding, and having snowball fights with their friends and family. They wake up the next morning and run to the window expecting to find a foot of snow, but sometimes all they find is sunshine. No snowball fights. No snowmen. No sledding.

Open your Bible and read Acts 27:25. Paul has been arrested and is being taken by ship to Rome. Winter is approaching, making for more dangerous weather and more unforgiving seas. As they travel, the wind picks up speed and becomes more powerful. The sky was so overcast that they couldn't see the sun or stars for many days, which was especially worrisome since sailors relied on the stars for navigation. But amidst all of the threats and dangers, Paul receives a message from God promising their safety.

Yes, meteorologists sometimes get their forecasts wrong. They make mistakes. They're only human, after all. But we must never assume that God is limited in the ways that humans are limited. God is omniscient — He knows all things — and this fact should give us courage. Like Paul, no matter what storms we face in this life, we must always remember that we can trust in God and have faith in His Word. There were soldiers and sailors on board the ship, men with authority and power and knowledge, but Paul took his direction from God and placed his faith in God's words rather than the words of men. And in the end, God's words proved true, and Paul made it to Rome in one piece. You can find courage in trusting God too.

REFLECT

1. WHEN DO YOU FIND IT MOST DIFFICULT TO TRUST GOD AND TAKE COURAGE IN HIM?

2. WHAT STORMS ARE YOU FACING IN YOUR LIFE RIGHT NOW?

3. WHAT STEPS HAVE YOU TAKEN TO HEAR FROM GOD DURING TIMES OF DISCOURAGEMENT AND DIFFICULTY?

VERSE TWENTY TWO

I have told you these things, so that in me you may have peace. In this world you will have trouble. But take heart! I have overcome the world.

JOHN 16:33

Movies use it. Books use it. Songs use it. It's a classic foil for plots: miscommunication. I thought you meant that when you said this. I didn't know that was how you felt. And it doesn't just happen in the movies. Misinterpretation is a catalyst for our own lives. The full story is sometimes difficult to come by, and we're left with only half (which we think is all). We begin to assume things — incorrect things — because we've misinterpreted.

Assumptions are frequently made about Scripture and the things that Jesus said. Some people think that when you become a Christian, everything just starts to line up for you. If you have enough faith, you can get that car, that house, that life that you've always wanted. Read John 16:33. Jesus is making no bones about it. He's speaking to His disciples for one of the very last times before His arrest. And He wants to impart some wisdom: This isn't gonna be easy. Life is hard. And it's about to get REAL HARD for some of you. BUT don't be afraid. Because in the end, I'm the one who wins this thing.

You can't really sugarcoat that. Jesus says it's going to be hard, and no manner of slick-haired, fast-talking pastor can change those words. You can't misinterpret that. And it's obvious that life is hard. Your best friend moves away. Your parents are getting a divorce. Your little brother has cancer. Life is hard. But as believers, we have a hope, and sometimes that hope is all we have to cling to. But it's enough. Because while Jesus doesn't mess around about life being hard, He also reminds us that He's with us and when all is said and done, He overcomes our hardships. And there's just no getting around it.

REFLECT

1. WHAT ARE SOME WAYS THAT PEOPLE HAVE MISINTERPRETED WHAT SCRIPTURE SAYS ABOUT THE LIFE OF A BELIEVER?

2. WHAT ARE THE HARDSHIPS IN YOUR LIFE?

3. ARE THE WORDS OF JESUS HERE IN JOHN 16:33 COMFORTING TO YOU? WHY OR WHY NOT?

VERSE 23

When they saw the courage of Peter and John and realized that they were unschooled, ordinary men, they were astonished and they took note that these men had been with Jesus.

ACTS 4:13

When Romans joined the military, typically around the age of sixteen, they received certain pieces of equipment. One piece of equipment was a helmet with a leather chin strap. Like a new pair shoes, the leather strap eventually softened as the soldiers wore it in. But despite the fact that the strap eventually softened, after years of wearing the helmet and after years of the leather rubbing against their skin, Roman soldiers were usually left with scars under their chins. The scar became a way for people to identify Roman soldiers, even if they weren't wearing their uniforms.

With that in mind, read Acts 4:13. Peter and John were on trial for miraculously healing a crippled beggar and preaching to the crowd of witnesses in Jerusalem. The priests, the captain of the temple, and the Sadducees arrested Peter and John for preaching the gospel, and the following day they were put on trial. After being questioned, Peter spoke up and did the very thing he was on trial for: He preached the gospel. He was bold and unashamed, and he spoke with wisdom and authority. This took everyone by surprise, and they could not deny that both Peter and John had been with Jesus. It's an awesome story; you should take a few minutes to read Acts 3:1–4:22.

Unlike Roman soldiers bearing scars under their chins, you probably don't have physical scars to reveal your identity and tell your story of faith (although many Christians suffering persecution in other parts of the world certainly do). But that doesn't mean you don't have a way of showing people that you've been with Jesus. Your lifestyle can reflect your relationship with Christ. Like Peter, your attitude and your words can boldly reveal to others, even those who don't yet have faith in Jesus, that you have been with the Lord.

REFLECT

1. WHAT ARE SOME WAYS IN WHICH YOU MAKE IT CLEAR TO OTHERS THAT YOU'VE BEEN WITH JESUS?

2. WHAT IN YOUR LIFE NEEDS TO CHANGE IN ORDER TO BETTER REFLECT YOUR RELATIONSHIP WITH CHRIST?

3. WHEN WAS THE LAST TIME YOU SHARED YOUR FAITH WITH OTHERS?

VERSE TWENTY FOUR

For I am not ashamed of the gospel, because it is the power of God that brings salvation to everyone who believes: first to the Jew, then to the Gentile.

Romans 1:16

Are you familiar with "herd mentality"? It's a term used to describe how people are often influenced by their peers to behave in a particular way. For instance, an individual might be compelled to buy a certain product simply because those at his or her work or school have bought the item. Herd mentality can be a good thing, especially in nature. Animals often stay huddled together in herds while traveling because there's safety in numbers. When it comes to people, though, the herd mentality sometimes takes a negative turn, like when it takes the form of peer pressure and leads to unsavory things, like drug use.

Grab your Bible and read Romans 1:16-17. In these verses, the Roman church is greeted with a wonderful statement of faith. Paul isn't ashamed of the gospel, and he's got the résumé to prove it. In his lifetime Paul goes hungry for the gospel, endures beatings for the gospel, is ostracized for the gospel, and eventually gives his life for the gospel. However, this isn't to say that Paul was never tempted to be ashamed of the gospel. In fact, it seems entirely possible that Paul wouldn't have felt compelled to include this statement if he hadn't, at one point or another, been tempted to be ashamed. Thankfully, we aren't held accountable for the temptations that assail us, only for what we do when we are tempted. Will we give in when we are tempted to be ashamed, or will we resist and be bold?

The herd isn't always going to line up with the teachings of Jesus. The majority won't always love the Lord like you love Him, or wish to please Him the way you wish to please Him. It's in such moments that we'll discover the depth of our faith. Like Paul, we ought to remain unashamed of our faith even when, or especially when, those around us are angered by it or think it's stupid.

reflect

1. In the past, what are some ways you have modified your behavior and lifestyle to match the herd?

2. Nowadays, what do you do when the herd doesn't love or value what you love and value?

3. List several reasons why it is more important to please Christ than it is to please others.

verse 25

Do not be overcome by evil, but overcome evil with good.

ROMANS 12:21

A few pages ago we mentioned the shocking reality that millions upon millions of people, including children, are being trafficked as slaves, even in the United States. There are approximately 950 million hungry people in the world. That means roughly one in seven people doesn't have the luxury of eating until they're full. About 6 million children die annually from malnutrition. Around 1 billion people don't have access to safe sources of water, leading to 5 million deaths each year from water-borne diseases.

Open your Bible and read Romans 12:21. In his travels Paul has seen good and evil, the best in people and the worst in people. He has seen people remain faithful to Christ, and he has seen people overcome by evil desires. Throughout his letter to the church in Rome, Paul has given detailed instructions for how to live out their faith, how to interact with each other, and how to deal with outsiders who hate them. Now he writes a single sentence that seems to sum it all up. He encourages them to overcome the evils of the world with the good placed in them by God. Every encouragement and every warning in the book of Romans comes down to this.

There is no shortage of evil in this world, and sometimes it can become overwhelming. When we catch ourselves feeling swamped by evil urges or by heartbreaking statistics, we must remember Paul's words. We don't have to be victims of evil desires. We don't have to remain spectators of the evil around us. God's goodness lives inside of us, and He has made a way for us to be statistic-changers. Don't be a victim or spectator of the evils around you. Instead, use the goodness God placed inside of you to overcome.

REFLECT

1. WHAT WILL YOU DO TO TAKE A BITE OUT OF THESE STATISTICS (OR OTHER EVILS AROUND YOU)?

2. WHO ARE THE PEOPLE IN YOUR LIFE WHO COULD USE A HAND IN OVERCOMING EVIL, WHETHER A FRIEND STRUGGLING WITH PORNOGRAPHY OR A NEIGHBOR LIVING IN POVERTY?

3. WHAT EVILS IN YOUR OWN LIFE NEED TO BE SURRENDERED TO GOD'S GOODNESS?

VERSE TWENTY SIX

Have I not commanded you? Be strong and courageous. Do not be afraid; do not be discouraged, for the Lord *your God will be with you wherever you go.*

JOSHUA 1:9

A news story came across the wire recently about a young Ethiopian girl who was kidnapped as she walked home from school. These men wanted to force this twelve-year-old girl into marriage, and during her kidnapping, she was beaten and abused. Most stories like these end with the girl being taken to a different city and becoming the wife/slave of someone she has never met. Not this time. Strangely, three lions emerged from the forest near where she was being held and chased the kidnappers away. The little girl, traumatized and alone, began to cry, sure that at any moment, the lions would attack her and she would die. But they didn't. They guarded her for hours, waiting to leave until the police found her, and then disappeared back into the forest.

Turn to Joshua 1:9 and read the verse. Moses has just died and Joshua is set to take over, to bring the Israelites into the Promised Land, but it won't be easy getting there. There will be hardship after difficulty after letdown. But before they begin, God wants to remind Joshua of something: DO NOT BE AFRAID; I WILL BE WITH YOU. The great promise that God delivers to Joshua, in the midst of what seems to be an overwhelming situation, is that He will be there.

This promise is not unfamiliar to most of us, but it's a hard one to let sink in. We read that God is with us, but do we know it in our bones? We have seemingly impossible odds to overcome, and maybe you think that this is actually the one time that God can't handle the mess you've made. You're wrong. Just like the girl who was guarded by the lions, God's presence may come in strange ways. And He is always with you; you do not have to be afraid of the unknown or the unclear. You have God and He is there.

REFLECT

1. WHAT ARE THINGS THAT YOU FEAR OR ARE DISCOURAGED BY?

2. WHY IS IT HARD TO KNOW THAT GOD IS NEAR, THAT YOU DON'T NEED TO BE AFRAID?

3. WHAT ARE SOME WAYS YOU'VE FELT GOD'S PRESENCE IN THE PAST?

VERSE 27

We are hard pressed on every side, but not crushed; perplexed, but not in despair; persecuted, but not abandoned; struck down, but not destroyed.

2 CORINTHIANS 4:8-9

According to the CIA World Factbook (yes, it's a real thing), the average American will live to be 78.37 years old. So if you were born in 1995, you might die around 2073. Now, maybe as a teenager that doesn't sound too bad, but how many times have you heard an older person say that time goes by faster the older you get? Plus there are all these things threatening your life: cancer, crime, car accidents, war, and terrorism. People die all the time before they reach the "average" age. We are fragile beings and our time on this earth is short. However, our tenure on this earth is not something we have to worry about.

Read 2 Corinthians 4:6-9. This letter was written in the first century when clay jars were used for everything. If one broke, it was no big deal. They used clay jars like we use Ziploc sandwich bags. Paul says our bodies are like Ziploc bags — easily torn and discarded. We are strong one day and worn out the next, but that's OK because our value is not based on our outward appearance. Paul says our Ziploc-bag selves are holding something extremely valuable inside. That treasure inside us is Jesus Christ — the one who brings hope.

Are you going to have some hard times in life? Yes. There will be times when you may not feel like living anymore, but keep going. Your Ziploc bag may be torn, dirty, and look like trash, but God holds on to you. When you follow Christ, you have a treasure inside you that makes you extremely valuable to God. A day will come when you won't need that sandwich bag shell, and your treasure will live for eternity. Hang in there! He is with you every step of the way.

REFLECT

1. WHAT ARE SOME THINGS IN YOUR LIFE RIGHT NOW THAT MAKE YOU FEEL TORN? IN OTHER WORDS, WHAT ARE SOME HARD THINGS YOU'RE FACING?

2. SPEND A FEW MINUTES PRAYING. ASK GOD TO GIVE YOU STRENGTH AND COURAGE TO KEEP GOING EVEN THOUGH YOU MAY BE DOWN PHYSICALLY OR EMOTIONALLY.

3. EVEN THOUGH YOU ARE FRAGILE, HOW CAN YOU SHOW THE STRENGTH OF GOD AND THE TREASURE OF CHRIST INSIDE YOU TO THE WORLD?

VERSE TWENTY EIGHT

But he said to me, "My grace is sufficient for you, for my power is made perfect in weakness." Therefore I will boast all the more gladly about my weaknesses, so that Christ's power may rest on me.

2 Corinthians 12:9

Do you know who Kevin Clash is? You've probably heard his voice and seen him perform on *Sesame Street* too many times to count. Kevin Clash is the puppeteer and voice of Elmo. Did you know that Elmo was not always a lovable, imaginative monster? Before 1985, Elmo had a deep caveman voice. Three other puppeteers tried to give life to Elmo, but it never seemed quite right. It wasn't until Kevin Clash started playing around with the furry red puppet that Elmo became known and loved by kids today.

Read 2 Corinthians 12:7-10. We often think of Paul as a great saint, but that wasn't always the case. Paul had his problems too. He didn't look nice (remember he had been stoned and gone to jail several times), he wasn't always the best speaker, and sometimes he spoke his mind a little too much, which made people mad. Some people in the Corinthian church thought that Paul's weaknesses were an embarrassment to the church. They didn't want him around because he just wasn't good enough. In verse 9, Paul tells his critics that while they view his problems as a humiliation to the church, Christ sees them as an opportunity.

Whether we know it or not, we are broken people. We have our flaws, whether physical or spiritual, but Jesus loves us anyway. Elmo is just plastic eyes and shaggy red cloth. He can't do anything but look cute. BUT, when Kevin Clash works with him, Elmo becomes a real monster kids can relate to and love. God is not bothered by your weaknesses. He knows you are messed up! He wants you to trust that He is able to use you in spite of your weaknesses. You have to be humble enough to allow Him to do that. When you are, God can use you to change the world around you.

reflect

1. What are some things you don't like about yourself? What are you doing that you know you shouldn't be doing?

2. Spend some time confessing your weaknesses to God. He knows them, but He just wants to make sure you know them too.

3. Ask God to use you to show His love to someone else today.

verse 29

"Not by might nor by power, but by my Spirit," says the Lord Almighty.

ZECHARIAH 4:6B

I remember being in elementary school, well before I had my first job, and desperately wanting to buy a Christmas present for my mom. But how are kids supposed to buy presents for their parents when they aren't making any money? Every year at Christmas my elementary school would set up a miniature store in one of the classrooms and allow students to come and purchase gifts for their parents. The gifts were small and cheaply made, but at least they were affordable on a fourth grader's salary. My mom used to give me a few dollars, and I would take the money and pick her out something for Christmas.

Open your Bible and read Zechariah 4:6. Zechariah is part of an effort to rebuild the temple, but at this point in time the work has been brought to a standstill. It's easy to imagine that Zechariah, being the leader of this important assignment, would feel overwhelmed with his duty and maybe even discouraged now that work was halted. In this verse Zechariah receives the encouragement and motivation that he needs. He's been woken from his sleep by an angel and been reminded that the task before him will be completed with God's help.

God doesn't tell Zechariah that he's good enough, strong enough, or smart enough to complete the rebuilding of the temple. God doesn't tell Zechariah to rely on the people around him, or on others' wealth, influence, and power. God tells Zechariah that this task will be completed by the Spirit of God. It all depends on God. Just like when I was in elementary school and couldn't even give my mom a Christmas present without first receiving the money from her, we can't give anything to God or do anything for God apart from His Spirit working in and through us.

REFLECT

1. WHEN ARE YOU TEMPTED TO RELY ON YOUR OWN MIGHT AND POWER RATHER THAN GOD'S SPIRIT?

2. WHO OR WHAT IN YOUR LIFE DO YOU TURN TO BEFORE TURNING TO GOD?

3. WHAT EFFORTS CAN YOU MAKE TO REMIND YOURSELF DAILY OF GOD'S POWER AND YOUR DEPENDENCE ON HIS SPIRIT?

VERSE THIRTY

I can do all this through him who gives me strength.
PHILIPPIANS 4:13

Bad, unexpected things happen. You straight A students will get a bad grade. One day you will get in a wreck and it will probably be your fault. Your best friend might move away, you may fight with your parents, you may get fired from your job or flunk out of college. Bad things happen sometimes (I know this is a little depressing, but stay with me). What are you going to do when that really bad day, week, month, or year happens?

Read Philippians 4:11-13. Paul has had some really bad times. He has been stoned to the point where his executioners thought he was dead. He has been shipwrecked, beaten, and even some of his friends have turned against him. He is writing this letter to the Philippians from jail! Paul is having a really bad time while he's writing these words down, but he doesn't seem to be discouraged. Why? Because after all these bad things happened, Paul has realized that God has everything under control. "I'm starving a little bit? No problem, God will feed me eventually. These chains are killing my wrist? It won't last forever." Paul has complete trust in what God can and will do.

When was the last time you freaked out because something didn't work out the way you planned? Why did you freak out? Did you think your discomfort would never end? Did you think all hope was lost? Hey! Paul is telling you not to lose hope! God has everything under control. You can endure any bad day. You can brush off any insults. You don't need to fall apart when your life is falling apart because nothing is impossible with God. Just don't forget who has your back. Thank Him every day for the strength He gives you.

REFLECT

1. HOW HAS GOD USED A BAD SITUATION IN YOUR LIFE TO TEACH YOU AND BLESS YOU? DO YOU THINK HE COULD DO THAT AGAIN?

2. ARE YOU GOING THROUGH A BAD TIME RIGHT NOW? WRITE DOWN SOME WAYS GOD IS GIVING YOU STRENGTH TO KEEP GOING.

3. SPEND SOME TIME THANKING GOD FOR GIVING YOU STRENGTH. ASK HIM TO SHOW YOU HOW HE IS HELPING YOU TODAY.

VERSE 31

Now to him who is able to do immeasurably more than all we ask or imagine, according to his power that is at work within us, to him be glory in the church and in Christ Jesus throughout all generations, for ever and ever! Amen.

EPHESIANS 3:20–21

"Whoa . . . What does this mean?!?!?!" This was the now-infamous question, gasped between sobs on one of the most famous viral videos in recent years. You know what I'm talking about. "Double-rainbow." This poor guy's mind was completely blown in 2010 by the overwhelming beauty of not one but two massive arches of color "all the way across the sky." What were the odds of such a rare display of natural wonder? "It's so intense." But for as many times as he cried, "Oh my God!" it's probably safe to say that this awestruck hippie had no idea that God really is the one responsible for all the wonders of Creation . . . and the best is still to come.

Two thousand years ago, the apostle Paul didn't have YouTube, but he did have parchment paper. One of his letters — what we now call Ephesians — was written and passed around to churches all over the ancient world. This "circular letter" as it was called was about as close to a viral video as the culture got back then. What's incredible is that Paul stops in the middle of this letter, almost as if he's overwhelmed by God's majesty, feeling very small in God's presence, to say a prayer. Grab your Bible and read Ephesians 3:14-21.

"Whoa . . . What does this mean?!?!?!" God has awesome things planned for your life. Literally awesome. We can't even begin to wrap our finite minds around the infinite power and goodness of God. We are all a part of His greater story of bringing salvation to every nation and generation in history. His Spirit is inside of you, empowering you to bring glory to Christ. Be overwhelmed by His love. But don't let it paralyze you. Let His incredible love and power motivate you to take action today.

REFLECT

1. WHEN HAVE YOU FELT OVERWHELMED BY GOD'S GLORY AND GREATNESS?

2. HOW DOES IT CHANGE THE WAY YOU SEE THE WORLD WHEN PAUL WRITES, "EVERY FAMILY IN HEAVEN AND ON EARTH DERIVES ITS NAME" FROM GOD THE FATHER?

3. HOW WILL YOU GLORIFY GOD IN YOUR GENERATION, LETTING THE LOVE, POWER, AND ABUNDANT LIFE OF CHRIST OVERFLOW FROM YOUR HEART THROUGH FAITH?

You made it!

This is a great step (or 31 great steps) in the right direction.

Following Christ is a journey. And don't let anyone tell you it's a walk in the park, either. It's not all double-rainbows, as you've seen.

It won't always be easy. It's actually going to get really tough at times. Life is hard. Life hurts. But our God is greater, and we have a greater reward in our eternal home than any passing pain or pleasure in this world. This world has nothing to compare to His glorious riches.

Hopefully, you've seen how valuable it is to spend time in God's Word and in prayer as you live these truths out each day. This little book is not the answer to life's questions and struggles. The Bible has everything you need to know, but the point of these devotions is to help you see life through a spiritual lens. By looking at life and Scripture each day, our hope is that you've developed a habit of being in conversation with God.

Talking. Listening. Living.

Walking with Christ, led by His Spirit.

Hopefully you've learned how to live in His presence, trusting in His power.

God has awesome things in store for you—plans that are already in motion.

Never settle for anything short of God's best. Give Him the glory He undoubtedly deserves.

Be on your guard; stand firm in the faith; be courageous; be strong.

Be . . .

AUDACIOUS.

ACKNOWLEDGMENTS

This book is the result of audacious Christ-followers using their unique God-given abilities, passions, and perspectives to help you better know Christ through His Word. Without the commitment and talent of the following people, this helpful little book wouldn't exist. So be encouraged, knowing that all kinds of different people are used by God to share their creative and technical skills for something bigger than themselves.

AUTHORS

Sean Bess
Jeremy Maxfield
Erin Moon
Josh Thompson

SENIOR EDITOR

Jeremy Maxfield

COPYEDITOR

Amanda Maxfield

GRAPHIC DESIGN

Katie Beth Owens